HIDDEN NAPLES
AND THE
AMALFI COAST

Massimo Listri

HIDDEN NAPLES AND THE AMALFI COAST

Text by Cesare Cunaccia

Special thanks to: Chiara Barracco and Tullia Gargiulo; Mauro Giancaspro, director of the National Library; and Michele Iodice, director of the National Archeological Museum.

Page 2
Detail of the wrought iron gates of the zoo.
Pages 4–5
Crater of Vesuvius at full moon, eruption of 1820.
Gouache on paper, San Martino National Museum.
Pages 6–7
Gatti and Dura, *Moonlight over the Eruption of 1858* (detail).
Gouache on paper, San Martino National Museum.

Translation: Judith Goodman
Graphics: Marcello Francone
Layout: Antonietta Pietrobon
Editorial Coordination: Cristina Sartori

First published in the United States of America in 2002 by
Rizzoli International Publications, Inc.
300 Park Avenue South
New York, NY 10010

© 2002 by Rizzoli Libri Illustrati
Società Editoria Artistica SpA
Gruppo Skira

2002 2003 2004 2005 2006 / 10 9 8 7 6 5 4 3 2 1

All rights reserved.
No part of this publication may be reproduced in any manner whatsoever without permission in writing from Rizzoli International Publications, Inc.

Library of Congress Control Number: 2002106883

ISBN: 0-8478-2482-9

Printed in Italy

Contents

10 Introduction

24 The Mystery of Religion in Naples

44 The Many Faces of Naples: Nativity Scenes and Pulcinella

62 From the Baroque to the Age of Illuminism

86 Ancient Splendors in the Steps of the Bourbons

102 The Love of Collecting

130 The Villas and Gardens of Capri and Sorrento: Nature and Myth

Introduction

It certainly is not easy to add anything to that grand, opulent, and vibrant book that is Naples. More than a city, Naples is a universe of opposites: it is a place blessed with great beauty and breathtaking landscapes, but it is equally dark and grungy, as southern Italian cities frequently are. Naples is aristocratic and ragamuffin, open and inviting, and, at the same time, unruly and secretive. Naples is at once Greek, Roman, and Byzantine; it is of Anjou and Aragon, of Pontano's Renaissance city and of Sannazaro. It is a city of great highs and lows: beset by plagues and revolts, and decorated with the most accomplished examples of painting, all golden and sumptuous, regal and stately.

The baroque essence of Naples is suspended between an air of a permanent feast day and the catharsis of Counter-Reformation meditation. It is a place where high art mingles with the most loathsome revelry of carnivals. Dominique Fernandez's magnificent *Pearls and Croissant* provides an apt description of Naples's contradictions. He writes: "Naples is resistant to bourgeois order, yet all of the city is baroque, the Bourbon quarter of Spaccanapoli,

Detail of the decorative sculpture behind the altar of the church of Santa Maria delle Anime del Purgatorio (St. Mary of the Souls in Purgatory).

the popular quarter of Toledo and Sanità, the aristocratic area of Pizzafalcone and Chiaia, the hundreds of palazzos, the 257 churches, the 57 private chapels set aside for vespers, the 182 chapels belonging to the confraternities, the 52 monasteries and the 24 convents. But there is also Baroque in the psychological fragility of the inhabitants, the very theatricality of each moment of existence."

There are few cities in the world where nature has the same spectacular power and energy. Perhaps only Genoa or Rio de Janeiro rival its natural wonders. In Naples nature and history are closely linked, and the landscape reveals the city's grand history. The unforgettable panorama from Villa Lucia—with its traces of the Bourbon Duchess of Partanna—is visible from the hill of Posillipo or from Parco Grifeo. One marvels at the islands, peninsulas, rocky coastlines; and above it all, Vesuvius rises solemnly.

The landscape bears the mark of the history it has experienced. It is the ground of Homer and Virgil and is therefore imbued with classical roots. In the city's enormous grottoes and in the necropolis one sees the evidence of the terrible and periodic waves of the plague. At the beginning of the nineteenth century, Madame de Staël followed in the footsteps of her heroine, Corinna, and found in Naples "a dreamy indolence," a sort of overabundance of soul that is one part mad enthusiasm and one

Horn-shaped good luck charms in a shop in Spaccanapoli.

part melancholy. In 1817 the great Stendhal was impressed by the archeological excavations at Pompeii, and he confided that "it is a real pleasure to see face to face that antiquity about which I have read volumes."

He also found unusual effects and systems of defense against the "evil eye." While visiting Don Nardo, an illustrious Neapolitan lawyer, Stendhal was greatly impressed by an oversized horn, about ten feet high, which was a lightning rod against the "evil eye." It was a simple precursor of those horns that appear today in shiny red bunches at the doors of the shops in San Gregorio Armeno.

Naples is surrounded by the brilliant blue of the Tyrrenian sea, that reaches as far as the island of Ischia and to the legendary island of Capri with its Dolomitic hills beloved by so many artists and writers. And the sea hugs the breathtaking Amalfi coast, from which one can see the islands of the Sirenuse. But the city is also capable of turning its back on the coastline, closing in upon itself like a wounded animal, and canceling out the sound of the waves and the life-giving breeze from the sea.

It is characterized by loud colors and even louder noise from the streets that are crammed with people and cars. It is a permanent carnival, constantly animated, very theatrical, and wholly unique and idiosyncratic. Dominique Fernandez has observed how the "magnificent palazzo of Cellamare outlines the border between the Naples of the sea and the more European

Detail of the marble decoration in the church of San Lorenzo Maggiore.

bourgeois areas on the one hand, and that suffocating and suffocated oriental region of the baroque areas." Pier Paolo Pasolini used to say that Naples would never change. And he was correct. Even if times change, the essence of the city—its carnivalesque mood—remains the same.

Naples is known for its musical history, both contemporary and historical. The songs of the 1950s by the sublime Roberto Murolo, an elegant and accomplished artist, continue to delight us. Long before Murolo, however, Naples was a center for opera, particularly in the eighteenth century. Masters such as Vinci, Traetta, Porpora, Durante, Jommelli, with Gianbattista Pergolesi, spread Neapolitan music around the conservatories of Europe. Naples vied with Venice for the title of "most important city in music"; both cities were home to musicans who were responsible for important musical innovations.

Porporino, or the Mysteries of Naples, a novel by the Dominique Fernandez, started a series of literary efforts dedicated to the theme of the *castrati* and a general depiction of the splendors and miseries of the city during the Bourbon reign. Porporino is dominated by that ambiguous prince Raimondo Sansevero di Sangro. He was a noxious character, an aristocratic scientist-cum-sorcerer of the Frankenstein genre. He is a figure now likened to Voltaire, a free thinker and freemason. Today it is suspected that he was secretly involved in the Inquisition and that

The Palace at Caserta, designed by Luigi Vanvitelli and begun in 1751.

he was a secret informer for the Jesuits. He was excommunicated by Pope Benedict XIV after the publication of his subversive *Lettera Apologetica*, and what is worse for a Neapolitan gentleman, he was excluded from the assembly of deputies of the Treasure of San Gennaro.

Spaccanapoli divides the historic center of Naples in two and corresponds to *Decumano Inferiore* which, like that of *Decumano Superiore* (present day Via dei Tribunali) dates back to Roman times. Looking down from the hill of San Martino, it is a long, narrow fissure that stretches as far as the area of Forcella. It is inhabited by people of every tradition, custom, and religion. It is the most authentic part of the city, where every kind of building can be found, from noble houses to convents. Spaccanapoli is the fortress where all the ancient spirits find refuge from the clamor and bright neon lights of progress. It is the shelter for the "little monk," a figure comparable to the Brazilian Preto Velho: capricious, full of jokes and malicious tricks. Meanwhile the people perform rites against bad luck and try to capture good fortune by entrusting themselves to a lottery booth, having first consulted *Smorfia*. This vital manual contains interpretations of dreams, which are then assigned numbers to be played on the lottery.

The art of the Nativity scene has been preserved at San Giorgio Armeno. As mentioned above, great artists of the

Detail of a bas-relief on the staircase at the Academy of Fine Arts.

eighteenth century such as Sammartino and Vaccaro and even King Charles III himself made Nativity scenes. The king loved to make and dress the pastoral figurines and the countless picturesque elements. (The molds used for the figurines date back to the seventeenth century.) So important were these crafts that there was a "hospital" of sorts devoted to fixing them in San Biagio dei Librai. Two centuries ago it "healed" puppets, mannequins, masks, and dolls.

The influence of Charles III is still evident in Naples and the surrounding area. He was the son of Elizabeth Farnese and Philip V of Spain. Crowned in 1735, he favored secular architecture over religious buildings. The superb San Carlo Theater was created by him. It was built between March and October 1737 by Angelo Carasale based on a design by Giovanni Antonio Medrano, and inaugurated on November 4 of the same year with "Achilles in Sciro" by Metastasio. In 1738 the king inaugurated the first official season of excavations at Herculaneum. He commissioned two important architects of the time to build a number of projects. Luigi Vanvitelli designed the plans for the Caroline Forum, and in 1751 began the construction of the Palace at Caserta. It was a marble building, very regular and symmetrical in design. It was an immense building heavy with symbols, both joyous and melancholy; It was never completed. "The kingdom of Naples is like the palace of Caserta," said the

Detail of Islamic-inspired decoration inside the Casa Rosa at Anacapri.

Prince of Salina in *The Leopard* by Giuseppe Tomasi di Lampedusa, "The architecture is magnificent, the furniture disgusting."

Vanvitelli also designed the Villa Campolieto, a characteristic suburban residence that rises in an area of other splendid residences and gardens at least a mile from the Reggia di Portici. This palace was commissioned by the Duke of Casacalenda in 1755 and built by Mario Gioffredo. Work was interrupted due to the periodic eruptions of Vesuvius, but it was eventually completed in 1775. The white embrace of the elliptical portico, which has only recently been restored after years of abandonment, is a testimony to the Miglio d'Oro, or Golden Mile. At least 120 villas of historical interest can be found on the slopes of Vesuvius. They are part of an historical and archeological heritage that dates back to Roman times and have been documented in art and literature from Tischbein to Leopardi, from Pitloo to Gigante.

It is, however, Vesuvius, "Vesevo the Exterminator," that dominates the whole area with its grumbling and intimidating presence. The terrible eruption of August 24, 79 A.D. destroyed Pompeii, Herculaneum, Stabia, and Oplontis. The last terrifying proof of the vitality of the volcano occurred in March 1944, which threw the Allied forces into disarray just as they had reached Naples. In the shadow of Vesuvius, Sir William Hamilton fell in love with the beautiful Emma Lyon; She was a celebrated neoclassical beauty and he the unfortunate husband. The volcano is the subject of the paintings of Vernet and souvenir gouaches for travelers on the Grand Tour. It is the subject of two diverse literary works, one by Norman Lewis entitled *Naples '44* and the other *The Skin* by Curzio Malaparte. And of course there was a series of works by Andy Warhol for the *Terrae Motus* exhibition, conceived by Lucio Amelio.

Massimo Listri has given the reader exquisite photography that tells the history of the city. His photographs tell of the intimate and intellectual Naples, and he manages to organize and render comprehensible the chaotic disorder of Naples. *Hidden Naples* is a wondrous journey—as wondrous as the city itself—that chronicles this amazing place: its art, its literature, its landscape—in short, its beauty.

THE MYSTERY
OF RELIGION
IN NAPLES

Naples is a mysterious place, a city which is home to strange and fascinating, inexplicable happenings. A site which embodies the mystery of the city is the Villa of the Mysteries at Pompeii, with the cycle of paintings that decorate the triclinium—a dining room with three couches—which depicts arcane religious rituals.

Mystery also shrouds the patron saint of Naples, San Gennaro. On the feast day of San Gennaro, September 19, two vials of the saint's blood liquefy to the incredible delight of the crowd. For the populace of Naples, it is an event not to be missed. (Neapolitans believe that if the blood liquefies on the two feast days, good luck will bless the city.) The cemetery of the Fontanelle, above the popular quarter Sanità, contains skeletal remains dating back to the sixteenth century and has macabre grottoes crowded with hundreds of skulls and bones. Naples has a long tradition of simple cults and superstitious Neapolitans have long practiced old magical rites to ward off the "evil eye."

Sansevero Chapel is one of the wonderous places of Naples. It was built by Raimondo de Sangro VII, Prince of Sansevero. The grounds, as legend has it, were already haunted by the ghost of Carlo Gesualdo, prince of Venosa, a seventeenth-century gentleman, who, in 1590, murdered his wife, Maria d'Avalos, and her lover, Fabrizio Carafa, when he caught them together. The chapel is replete with allegorical emblems and also includes a particularly strange object: two skeletons complete with "working" blood circulation systems. Less bizarre objects include extraordinary sculptures by Queirolo, Corradini, Celebrano. The sublime and disturbing *Veiled Christ* sculpted in 1753 by Giuseppe Sammartino reminds the viewer of the idiosyncratic character of the artist. His many varied pursuits included: alchemy, engineering, pyrotechnics, and magic.

Votive shrine in the crypt of the church of Santa Maria delle Anime del Purgatorio.

A bronze skull on the exterior of the church of Santa Maria delle Anime del Purgatorio and, right, a votive shrine on Vico Panettieri.

The charnel-house of the Fontanella in the heart of the Sanità quarter.

Old books in the archives of patrician Neapolitan families at the State Archives, and the window of a second-hand shop on Via dei Tribunali.

This page and following: The frescoes of Villa dei Misteri at Pompeii, details of the Dionysian frieze, theatrical mask, and Egyptian-inspired decoration.

This page and following: *The Veiled Christ* at the Sansevero Chapel, sculpted by Giuseppe Sammartino in 1753.

Details of the *Disillusionment* of Francesco Queirolo, known as *The Fisherman*, another of the sculptures inside the Sansevero Chapel.

Details of the tombs of Giovanni Francesco Paolo di Sangro and of Cecco di Sangro sculpted by Francesco Celebrano above the entrance to the Sansevero Chapel.

THE MANY FACES OF NAPLES: NATIVITY SCENES AND PULCINELLA

On Via San Gregorio Armeno, the shops teem with figurines and accessories for Nativity scenes all year round and not just during the Christmas season. This fact is enough to make one realize how deeply rooted the Nativity scene is in the Neapolitan soul and imagination. Eighteenth-century Nativity scenes are particularly beautiful—brilliantly sumptuous and very baroque, they are world famous. In the museum at the Certosa di San Martino there is a section entirely dedicated to the representation of the Nativity. It is primarily comprised of the work in the collection of Michele Cuciniello, who donated these and many other objects to the municipality in 1880 with the condition that the original eighteenth-century settings were to be preserved.

In the eighteenth century important sculptors like Vaccaro and Sammartino enjoyed dedicating their time to this extremely local art form. Meanwhile, the king, the court, the great aristocratic families, and the rich middle classes competed with each other to produce increasingly elaborate Nativity scenes. These were copied by ordinary people, who were also bewitched by the glorious magic that is associated with Christmas.

The character of Pulcinella, on the other hand, is a product of the Spanish quarters. Pulcinella is a character from the Commedia dell'Arte, and his form and personality were influenced by the Spanish. The famous mask—with its exaggerated features, including a large hook nose—represents the Neapolitan philosophy of survival, and also betrays a taste for sarcasm and irony. The character appeared for the first time on stage in 1601 in the theater company of Silvio Fiorillo. Pulcinella was melancholy and ill-mannered, romantic and sarcastic; sometimes his jokes were cruel, but he was infinitely tender. In his contradictions and many forms, Pulcinella has charmed the world, much as Naples has.

This and facing page and following: Details of the figures that crowd around the Nativity scene by Giuseppe Sammartino at Capodimonte.

50

52

This and facing page: Model of the ancient pharmacy in the Donatone collection.
Following pages: Pulcinella and Nativity statuettes in the windows of a shop on Via dei Tribunali.

This page: Two nineteenth-century Neapolitan ceramic plates featuring Pulcinella.
Facing page: A Neapolitan terra-cotta figure vase.

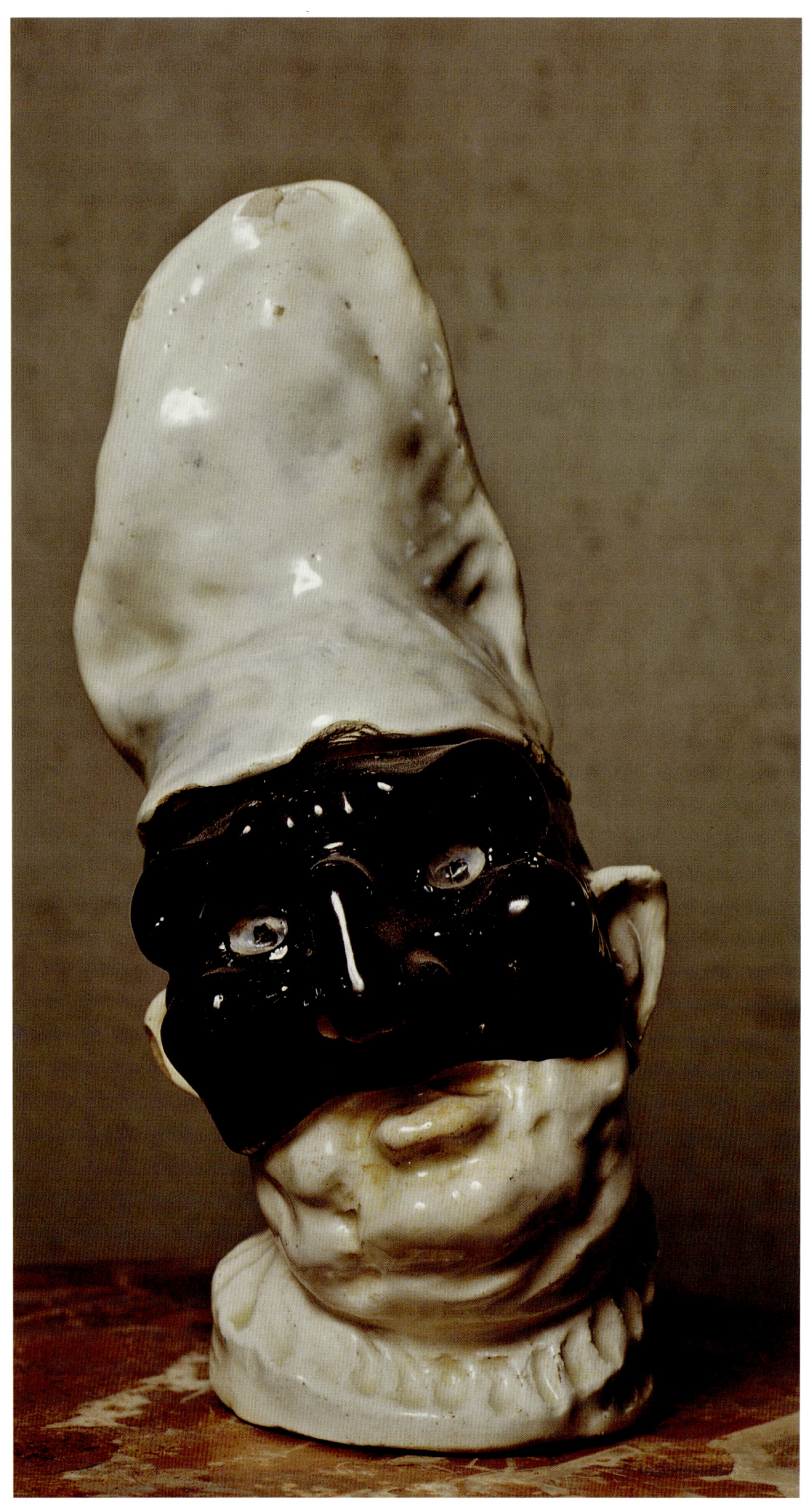

This and facing page: Pulcinella in polychrome terra-cotta, a wooden mold for a mask of Pulcinella from the end of the eighteenth century, and a nineteenth-century bust in terra-cotta.

61

FROM THE BAROQUE TO THE AGE OF ILLUMINISM

Naples is the quintessential baroque city. The Vice Regal period of the seventeenth century, with its many contradictions, was witness to terrific glory and unbelievable tragedy, of great celebrations and bloody riots. It is the century during which Cosimo Fanzago erected the superb pier on the water at the Palace Donn'Anna, for the consort of the Spanish Viceroy, don Ramiro Guzman Duke of Medina de las Torres. He also transformed the ancient Certosa di San Martino and the Cacace Chapel of San Lorenzo Maggiore into an exalted and theatrical place. Great artists of the period had a profound effect on the city, as they brought their considerable talents to the Neapolitan architecture, particularly the churches. Artists such as Caravaggio, Artemisia Gentileschi, Giovanni Lanfranco, Simon Vouet, and Vélasquez remade the city with their extraordinary art. There was a generation of noteworthy painters that were based in Naples, such as Bernardo Cavallino, Giovan Battista Caracciolo, and Massimo Stanzione. (Sadly, many of them were killed by the plague of 1656, a tragedy chronicled by Micco Spadari.) Mattia Preti, Ribera, the prolific Luca Giordano, and Francesco Solimena spread Neapolitan painting all over Europe.

Luigi Vanvitelli, the son of a Dutch landscape artist, was the main figure of local eighteenth-century architecture. The architect Ferdinando Sanfelice was also important in the city. He is known for his multileveled staircases that looked like stage scenery, and can be found in the sordid and dilapidated courtyards of Old Naples.

Mosaic of polychrome marble in the studio of Cosimo Fanzago in the church of San Lorenzo Maggiore.

This and facing page: Marble inlays and details of the sculptured decoration in the Cacace Chapel in San Lorenzo Maggiore from the studio of Cosimo Fanzago.

This page and following: Sculpted busts by Andrea Bolgi from 1653 for the Cacace Chapel in San Lorenzo Maggiore.

This and facing page: Bronze bust of Benedict XIII and two Apulian urns in the eighteenth-century salon of the Library of the Girolamini.

This page: The staircase with five vaults in the Palazzo dello Spagnolo.

Facing page: Open staircases in the courtyard of Palazzo Sanfelice.

This and facing page: Interior of the staircases of Palazzo Sanfelice and Palazzo dello Spagnolo.

This page: Detail of the service staircase at Palazzo Sanfelice.
Facing page: The entrance of a palazzo on Via Nilo, a crossroad of Spaccanapoli.

This and facing page: The stairway leading to the hanging garden of Palazzo Marigliano and the two majestic ramps of stairs at Palazzo Spinelli di Laurino.

Preceding, this page and facing: Details of the grand staircase and the elliptical portico of the villa of the Duke of Campolieto designed by Luigi Vanvitelli. This is one of the villas on the Golden Mile, the straight line between Herculaneum and Torre del Greco, which was once flanked by splendid villas with parks and gardens.

ANCIENT SPLENDORS
IN THE STEPS
OF THE BOURBONS

The Bourbon dynasty has left a vivid and omnipresent mark on the imagination and soul of Naples. It is a contradictory and fascinating thread of splendors and miseries: of illuminated government and total abandonment, absolutism and reforms denied and conceded, royal magnificence and plebeian spontaneity, cruelty and tenderness, pride and abject fear.

In 1860 with the accession of Charles III of Bourbon and the end of the Viceregal rule of Spain, the curtain finally fell on that which from 1735 had been the Kingdom of the Two Sicilies. This kingdom had lasted a little more than 130 years. These years were varied, fascinating, and complex, with reactions of wounded absolutism to philosophical, artistic, and musical splendors. There were attempts at liberty and consequent attempts to halt the inevitable, sensational decay of the ancien régime.

The arrival of Charles III marked an extraordinary debut for the Bourbons of Naples. On the European intellectual, artistic, social, and musical scenes, he brought the city to a point of rivalry with Paris, Venice, and London. His policy was reformist and illuminist, and he initiated an unequalled period of building renewal. The Palace at Caserta, with its splendid gardens, and the Palace at Portici, the royal seat of Cardito and Carditelli, were built during his rule. The Manufacture of Ceramics at Capodimonte and the silk factories of San Leucio were founded to provide an indigenous source for the luxury market. Excavations were initiated at Herculaneum and Pompeii, and a series of villas began to rise on the hill of Posillipo and the slopes of Mount Vesuvius. Unfortunately, Charles's heir, Ferdinand I, was not able to continue his father's work; he was forced into exile (under the protection of the English) in Sicily after the 1799 revolt of Naples and the proclamation of Joachim Murat as king. Restored in 1815, Ferdinand I carried out an internal repression, steering a course among the European powers with difficulty. Francis II, known as "Franceschiello," was weak and unlucky. He was eventually deposed, and in 1860 the Savoy dynasty was installed.

The throne room of the "New Apartment" at the Palace at Caserta. It is dominated by an allegorical figure holding a plaque dedicated to Ferdinand II.

The bedroom of Francis II and the queen's bathroom in the Palace at Caserta.

Caroline of Bourbon's bathroom at the Belvedere of San Leucio.

Above: A kneeling statue of Venus.
Facing page: Views of the English Garden on the grounds of the Royal Palace of Caserta.

Following pages, left: *Portrait of Maria Isabella of Bourbon* by Carlo De Fallo. The queen is also portrayed in the miniature that decorates the clock. Right: Painting of an interior of the palace of Naples, with Ferdinand II, and a salon in the royal palace. The oil painting is attributed to Frans Vervloet.

97

Pompeian sitting room in the historic apartment of the Palace of Capodimonte, with a table in alabaster and fossil wood in the center of the room.

Above: A terra-cotta bust of Ferdinand of Bourbon beside two fifth-century B.C. Attic vases decorated with red figures from Ruvo di Puglia.
Below: Bust of Antonio d'Este by Antonio Canova and a round, first-century B.C. pendant in white marble from Pompeii.

Clocks with Egyptian-inspired decoration produced in Naples at the beginning of the nineteenth century.

THE LOVE
OF COLLECTING

In 1777 Ferdinand I founded the Neapolitan Archeological Museum in the Palazzo degli Studi. There he decided to install the Farnese collection, which belonged to his paternal grandfather and was begun in 1547 by Alessandro Farnese, the future Pope Paul III. This exceptional collection consisted of many famous sculptures, including the group of the Farnese Bull and the Farnese Hercules, as well as those findings from Pompeii and Herculaneum that were kept in the palace at Portici.

The Bourbons' favorite residence in Naples was Capodimonte, which contained archeological remains of great importance, as well as sublime paintings. The palace, on the hill of the same name, was built by Antonio Medrano in 1738 for Charles III, to house the very rich collections of art that the enlightened monarch had inherited from his mother, Elizabeth, the last of the Farnese, lords of Parma. By marriage to a princess of Saxony, Charles also acquired the most precious secret of Philip August II: his porcelain. Charles ordered the architect Ferdinando Sanfelice to build the Royal Factory of Porcelain in the park of Capodimonte, where a large forest enabled the king to indulge his passion for the hunt. The famous Neapolitan ceramics created in this factory are now collected in the Duca di Martina National Museum of Ceramics.

Another museum that was born of a private, local collection is the Filangeri Civic Museum, which was seriously damaged in 1943 during World War II. This was the noble residence of Gaetano Filangeri. It was enriched by various donations and today houses a treasure of European and oriental weapons, medals, textiles, coins, porcelains, ancient parchment scrolls, and paintings, displayed in the eclectic and neo-Renaissance rooms of the building.

Facing and following pages: The depository of the Archeological Museum crowded with Roman sculptures from the Farnese collection.

This and facing page: The Academy of Fine Arts built by Enrico Alvino in 1863.

This and facing page: The staircase and the library of the Academy of Fine Arts.
Following page: One of the rooms of the National Library at the Royal Palace.

The room with the overhead gallery in the Filangeri Civic Museum. Greek vases and ceramics and porcelains from the most important Italian, European, and Far Eastern artisans are housed in the glass cases.

Facing page: The Library of Prince Gaetano Filangeri. This page: Some of the objects conserved in the Filangeri Civic Museum. Many of the objects donated to the city by Prince Gaetano Filangeri were destroyed in a fire set by German troops in 1943.

This, preceding, and following pages: Some pieces from the Donatone collection, which is comprised mostly of objects made in Naples from the sixteenth to the nineteenth centuries.
Preceding pages: Details of a small eighteenth-century Neapolitan cabinet by Gaspare Lopez and a seventeenth-century coin cabinet painted on glass.

Following pages: Left, two sixteenth-century profiles in marble and basalt.
Bottom right: The majolica room, with a group in terra-cotta with *Aurora's Chariot*, by Filippo Tagliolini standing on an eighteenth-century Neapolitan table in gypsum.

This, facing, and following pages: The collection of rare plants from the Botanical Gardens in the Royal Palace at Portici, seat of the Faculty of Agriculture.

129

THE VILLAS AND GARDENS OF CAPRI AND SORRENTO: NATURE AND MYTH

In the footsteps of those travelers on the Grand Tour, and an Italian itinerary first set out by Goethe, the islands of the Gulf of Naples and the coast became a pilgrimage ever more fashionable for legions of Nordic intellectuals and young people from good families. Self-satisfied ladies and gentlemen of doubtful reputations traveled the region, followed, towards the end of the nineteenth century, by eccentrics of every kind. Then came the political refugees and exiles who desired an escape from the censorship of respectable society.

Sorrento is a place of exquisite pictorial seduction, exemplified by the radiant beauty of the garden at Villa Tritone, built for Lord Astor at the end of the nineteenth century. The island of Capri was soon to take center stage on the international playground of misbehavior and eccentricity. Anacapri was chosen as home by an ex-captain of the Confederate Army, J. C. MacKowen. To make his archeological dream come true, MacKowen left the United States in 1876 and immersed himself in the inscriptions and marble fragments of classical sculptures. Like the garden of Lady Gordon Lennox at Monte San Michele, the classical myths can be experienced against a background of Mediterranean flora. Villa San Michele, created by the Swedish doctor, Alex Munthe, is a place to achieve a complete sense of belonging to the Mediterranean, as well as an understanding of the legend of this author.

This, facing, and preceding page: The citrus garden at Il Pizzo in Sorrento.

Villa Tritone stands on a steep cliff overlooking the Gulf of Sorrento. The villa looks out onto a marvelous Mediterranean garden that was enriched with many exotic plants by Lord Astor at the beginning of the twentieth century.

This and following pages: Views of the garden at Villa Tritone.

Views of the garden at Villa Falsitta, on Capri.

This, facing and preceding pages: Villa San Michele on Capri. It was built by Axel Munthe, a Swedish doctor and writer, who, like many other foreign travelers, fell in love with the island.

This and following page: Two views of the garden at Villa San Michele. During the construction of the villa, excavations brought to light Roman archeological remains that have been inserted into the building.

This page and following: The Ionic temple and garden of Monte San Michele on Capri, belonging to Lady Gordon Lennox.

Above: A nineteenth-century gouache depicting the Blue Grotto, which is still a source of fascination for tourists today as it was in centuries past.
Facing and following pages: The Casa Rossa in Anacapri. This is an antique seventeenth-century tower that was transformed into a villa at the end of the nineteenth century by the American J.C. MacKowen, who was passionate about Italy and archeology.

This and facing page: Two large canvases preserved in the museum at the Certosa di Capri. The paintings, *Sea Grotto* and *Capri Landscape,* are by Karl Wilhelm Diefenbach, a German painter who spent the last years of his life on Capri, from 1900 to 1913.

159